114 Tennis Strategies, Mental Tactics, and Drills Improve Your Game in 10 Days

By Joseph Correa

"Learn how to uncover mental and physical skills you never thought you had."

COPYRIGHT PAGE
© 2013 114 Tennis Strategies, Mental Tactics, and Drills
By Joseph Correa
ISBN 978-1-941525-06-7

All rights reserved. This book or any portion thereof may not be reproduced or used in any manner without the express written permission of the publisher except for brief book quotations for reviews in the book.

Scanning, uploading, and distributing of this book via the Internet or via any other means without the express permission of the publisher and author is illegal and punishable by law.

Only purchase authorized editions of this book. Please consult with your physician before training and using this book.
You can visit the author's website at tennisvideostore.com

INTRODUCTION

Strategy plays a big part in competitive tennis and knowing how to apply those strategies can help win more matches against tougher opponents.

These strategies will allow you to do three things:

1. Prepare for a specific style of player.
2. You will know what counter strategies can be used to most effectively compete.
3. How to execute those strategies based on your style of play.

This tennis strategy and mental tactics playbook is pocket size and should be kept in your tennis bag or where you will most likely see it to keep you ready to apply which ever strategy will be most useful for that match.
Point drills and advanced tennis drills are lots of fun and are exciting for the players doing them. Sometimes it might become difficult for you to complete some of the rope drills but don't give. Keep working hard and eventually you will get it right. This unusual type of training will help you to improve your overall control of high balls, low balls, high top spin, and low slice, flat or with minimal topspin. You will also improve your ability to direct the ball to specific spots on the court as well as become a lot more consistent. Once you complete this training you will feel more complete as a tennis player and will enjoy making your opponents work harder than they have ever before.

If you are beginner or intermediate in level, you can still do these drills as they can only make you better than you are right now but you might feel it requires some

persistence until you get it right.
Everything here is assuming you are right handed but you can simply do the opposite if you are left handed. This was done to simplify things but applies to both right handed players and left handed players.

ABOUT THE AUTHOR

Hello, my name is Joseph Correa and I have been training and teaching tennis for over 15 years. I played professional tennis for years and am now a USPTR professional certified coach.

After years of competing and training with some of the best in the world I have learned that most people can be very successful in competition with the right mental, physical, and emotional training.

Proven scientific techniques, drills, and step by step phases must be performed to reach your peak and for that reason I have prepared the first group of training DVD's and books showing you how to reach your goals.

Through my work and teaching aids, I have helped hundreds of amateur and professional tennis player's advance with their physical, mental, and performance goals to achieve great results.

I teach you everything I know you will need to reach your goals and hope you will enjoy and share these lessons and ideas with loved ones. To learn more about the different lessons taught through my books and DVD's go to www.tennisvideostore.com. Many more books will be coming out this year with some advanced drills and techniques.

TABLE OF CONTENTS

COPYRIGHT PAGE
INTRODUCTION
ABOUT THE AUTHOR
MATERIALS NEEDED AND SET UP

CHAPTER 1: STRATEGIES AGAINST BASIC STYLES OF PLAY
1. How to beat the baseliner
2. What to do against a net-rusher
3. How to beat the counter-puncher
4. How to beat the serve and volley player
5. How to out-play the all-court player
6. How to overcome the lobber
7. How to beat a pusher

CHAPTER 2: STRATEGIES AGAINST ADVANCED STYLES OF PLAY
8. What to do against a heavy topspin player
9. How to overcome the slice only player
10. How to overcome a big serve
11. How to counter a drop shot
12. How to overcome the runner
13. How to out-play a big forehand
14. How to overcome a big hitter

CHAPTER 3: STRATEGIES AGAINST UNSUAL STYLES OF PLAY
15. How to beat the grunter
16. How to beat the time delaying player
17. How to overcome a fast paced player
18. How to beat the crowd favorite
19. How to counter soft angles

20. How to counter deep and high shots
21. How to counter overcome high backhands
22. How to beat the scrap shot player

CHAPTER 4: MENTAL STRATEGIES
23. How to overcome nerves
24. How to overcome stress in a match
25. How to stay focused until the end
26. What to think during change-overs
27. What to think before a match
28. What to think the night before a match
29. What to do when you're a set down
30. What to do when you are a set up
31. What to do when you have match point
32. What to do after serving a double fault

CHAPTER 5: MENTAL TACTICS
33. "Know thy opponent"
34. "The match ends, when it ends"
35. "Prepare for success"
36. "Keep a poker face"
37. "Hide your weaknesses, exploit theirs"
38. "He who gets the last ball in, wins"
39. "Be true to thy self"
40. "He who hits first, hits twice"
41. "Be a fake to win"
42. "Bring down the walls"
43. "Learn from every match"
44. "Acquire Knowledge"
45. "Know thy rules"
46. "Build your chess board"
47. "Find the pattern"
48. "Pawn check mates king"
49. "Build a base"

50. "Don't dry up the well"
51. "Mind over matter"
51. "Only give presents on birthdays"
52. "Have the heart of a lion"
53. "Choose your weapon"
54. "Perfection by imitation"
55. "The four leaf clover"
56. "Humor for the brave"
57. Go where the party is at"
58. "Baby steps for giants"
59. "Thy second serve: may it serve you well"
60. "No jam, just bread and butter"

CHAPTER 6: FED DRILLS
1. Hitting over the rope cross court forehand
2. Hitting over the rope cross court backhand
3. Hitting over the rope down the line forehand
4. Hitting over the rope down the line backhand
5. Hitting over the rope alternating forehand and backhand cross court
6. Hitting over the rope alternating forehand and backhand down the line
7. Hitting under the rope cross court forehands
8. Hitting under the rope cross court backhands
9. Hitting under the rope down the line forehands
10. Hitting under the rope down the line forehands
11. Hitting under the rope alternating forehands and backhands cross court
12. Hitting under the rope alternating forehands and backhands down the line

CHAPTER 7: LIVE BALL DRILLS
OVER THE ROPE

13. Over the rope 20 balls with topspin forehand to forehand cross court rally (consistency)
14. Over the rope 20 balls with topspin backhand to backhand crosscourt rally (consistency)
15. Over the rope 20 balls with topspin forehand to backhand down the line rally (consistency)
16. Over the rope 20 balls with topspin backhand to forehand down the line rally (consistency)
17. Over the rope 20 balls with one person hitting only cross court while the other does down the line shots (figure 8 consistency)
18. Over the rope 20 balls with one person hitting only down the line while the other does cross court shots (figure 8 consistency)

UNDER THE ROPE DRILLS

19. Under the rope 20 balls cross court forehand to forehand rally
20. Under the rope 20 balls cross court backhand to backhand rally
21. Under the rope 20 balls down the line forehand to backhand rally
22. Under the rope 20 balls down the line backhand to forehand rally
23. Under the rope 20 balls cross court slice backhand rally
24. Under the rope 20 balls with one person hitting cross court while the other hits only down the line to create a figure 8
25. Under the rope 20 balls with one person hitting down the line while the other hits only cross court to create a figure 8

OVER AND UNDER THE ROPE DRILLS

26. One person hits forehands over the rope with topspin while the person hits forehands under the rope cross court
27. One person hits backhands over the rope with topspin while the person hits backhands under the rope cross court
28. One person hits forehands over the rope with topspin while the person hits backhands under the rope down the line
29. One person hits backhands over the rope with topspin while the person hits forehands under the rope down the line
30. One person hits backhands over the rope with topspin while the person hits slice backhands under the rope cross court
31. One person hits forehands over the rope with topspin while the person hits forehands under the rope crosscourt inside out

CHAPTER 8: POINT DRILLS

32. Points up the 10 only over the rope without serve
33. Points up to 10 only under the rope without serve
34. Points up to 10 where one person can only hit over the rope while the other can only hit under the rope without serve
35. Points up to 10 (with serve) over the rope (serve goes under the rope at all times unless you are doing a topspin or kick serve)
36. Points up to 10 (with serve) under the rope (serve goes under the rope at all times unless you are doing a topspin or kick serve)

CHAPTER 9: NORMAL POINT DRILLS WITHOUT ROPE

37. Points up the 10 without serve only cross court forehands

38. Points up to 10 without serve only cross court backhands

39. Points up to 10 without serve only down the line backhand to forehand

40. Points up the 10 without serve only down the line forehand to backhand

41. Points up the 10 with serve only cross court forehands

42. Points up to 10 with serve only cross court backhands

43. Points up to 10 with serve only down the line backhand to forehand

44. Points up the 10 with serve only down the line forehand to backhand

45. Points up to 10 where one person can only hit cross court and the other person can only hit down the line without serve

46. Points up to 10 where one person can only hit down the line and the other person can only hit cross court without serve

47. Points up to 10 where one person can only hit cross court and the other person can only hit down the line with serve

48. Points up to 10 where one person can only hit down the line and the other person can only hit cross court with serve

49. Points up to 10 without serve. Complete normal points without any patterns.

50. Points up to 10 with serve. Complete normal points without any patterns.

51. Play a complete set with serve playing only cross court while your partner hits only down the line.

52. Play a complete set with serve playing only down the line while your partner hits only cross court.
53. Play a complete set using any pattern you desire.
54. Play a complete match using any pattern you desire.
Would you do me a favor?
Other titles by Joseph Correa

MATERIALS NEEDED AND SETUP

You will need:
1 Tennis court
1 rope long enough to be tied to both ends of the court.
Someone to feed you balls and someone to hit balls back at you for that part of the training.
Set up:
Measure about 2-3 feet from the height of the net so that you can tie the rope about this height on both sides of the fence (or other object you can use to tie around). Take a ruler and measure 2 feet above the height of the net for advanced and 3 feet for normal difficulty.

CHAPTER 1: STRATEGIES AGAINST BASIC STYLES OF PLAY

Strategy #1
How to beat the baseliner

PROBLEM:
A good baseliner is comfortable at the baseline and would prefer not to go to the net. For this reason, the best strategy would be to bring the baseliner to the net with defensive shots where they will be in the worst situation and will probably get based or simply miss an easy volley.

SOLUTION:
One of the best ways to defeat a baseliner is to bring them into the net by hitting any of these shots: a short slice, a drop shot, a short topspin, a short angle.
If you hit a short slice the baseliner will be tempted to come into the net and if it's very short, he should be forced to leave the baseline and come forward to do a volley or overhead.

If you hit a drop shot, you will definitely be able to bring your opponent into the net as they will have no choice but to step inside the serving boxes at the net.
If you hit a short topspin shot, they won't be forced to come into the net but will be in a very bad position on the court if they don't. You can take advantage of their bad positioning by simply hitting behind them.
If you hit a short angle, they not only will be off the baseline but also slightly out of the court which would put them in a very bad position if they don't try to cover the court by coming into the net.

If you have a good serve, serve and volley or rush the net simply to surprise them and get some free errors every once in a while.

Strategy #2
What to do against a net-rusher

PROBLEM:

The net rusher is always ready to move forward mostly on second serves, weak shots and short balls. Their best shots are normally their volleys and overhead. They will rush the net after serving as well. They win most points by putting pressure at the net which forces errors or bad decisions from opponents.

SOLUTION:

The best solutions is to simply keep the net-rusher on the baseline by getting your first serve in, even of that means taking some power off and placing the ball instead. Also, hit deep topspin and cross-court to keep the net-rusher out of the court and away from the net.
If the net-rusher has reached the net you should plan to:

1. Pass them by hitting down the line.
2. Pass them by hitting crosscourt.
3. Pass them by hitting a short angle.
4. Lob the ball over their backhand side with a flat, topspin or slice shot.
5. Hit the ball straight at their body to keep them off guard and slow them down.

**Strategy #3
How to beat the counter-
puncher**

PROBLEM:
The counter-puncher is not the one to take the initiative during the point. They are usually the type of players that will wait for you to make a decision and then out-do your shot. If you rush the net they will pass you. If you attack by hitting harder they will use your power and play the open court. These types of players are big trouble when you don't know how to play them. The harder and faster you play the better it is for them if you don't have a concise strategy.

SOLUTION:
To beat the counter-puncher you need to understand that most of the time if you want to attack, you need to make sure you have a pattern beforehand that you can put into practice during the point.

 A few examples would be:

- Serve out wide and then hit to the open court.
- Hit to the open court and then follow your shot to the net to put more pressure on your opponent and close out the point.
- Hit a short ball and force them to take the initiative by coming into the net.

Strategy #4
How to beat the serve and volley player

PROBLEM:
Serve and volley players are fast and decisive. They will not blink when they have the opportunity to finish the point. They will serve a strong serve with power or spin and then follow it to the net.

SOLUTION:
The best strategy against this style of play is to slow them down or stop them as they come in.

The three best ways to slow them down and get them to make more errors are:

1. Return their serve to their feet so that they have to hit a half volley.

2. Return their serve right at their body as to make them have to turn their body out of the way to volley. This might not be a nice way to slow them down but it works and is another tool when you have no other options.

3. Lob them. Simply return the ball high and deep and then you should back up in case they decide to hit a hard overhead in the air as many will try to do this. If you hit a high enough lob they will have to stop completely and hit a well-timed overhead that is not always easy when it's windy, rainy, mid-day and the sun is right in their eyes or at night when it's most difficult to distinguish distances.

Strategy #5
How to out-play the all-court player

PROBLEM:
The all-court player can do it all. Serve and volley, counter-punch, chip and charge the net, be patient and consistent on the back court. Everyone is always practicing and working hard to become an all-court player so that you don't have any obvious weaknesses which would make it easier for you opponent to attack.

SOLUTION:
The all-court player is usually good at everything but that does not mean they don't have weaknesses. Focus on what they do worst and adjust the match so that you are doing what you do best.

For example: if they have a weaker backhand and you have a strong forehand, you should serve to their backhand and then run around your backhand as to hit a forehand. Continue putting pressure by hitting to their backhand until you get the opportunity to come to the net and or to put the ball away. This way you force them to play your most effective style of play against their weakest shot. Another good strategy would be to attack the net on their weaker side and force them to make errors this way.

**Strategy #6
How to overcome the lobber**

PROBLEM:
Players who lob the ball or hit high moon balls over and over again can be very difficult to play against and can make you lose your patience. You want to attack but they simply slow everything down with their lobs. When you want to come into the net you know you're going to have to hit an overhead.

SOLUTION:
You don't want to lose a match because you're going for low percentage shots while your opponent is hitting percentage shots such as lobs. They best plan would be to get them out of their comfort zone and force them to hit lobs from bad positions on the court or in locations that do not allow them to lob. By hitting low angled shots you will force lobbers to step out of the back court and to the sides which makes for a much harder lob since the distance to the backcourt is short than if they were standing far behind the baseline. Another way to get these types of players out of their lobbing game is to simply hit a short ball or drop shot as to bring them into the net. At the net you can either volley or hit an overhead, but no lobs! Another effective way to beat lobbers is to hit low short slices as it is much harder to hit a decent lob of a shot like that and then you can simply hit behind them after they return a not so good lob. The last option you have against a lobber is to hit the ball in the air so that the ball never bounces. This can be very effective if you're standing inside the baseline and feel comfortable swinging at balls in the air.

**Strategy #7
How to beat a pusher**

PROBLEM:

"Pushers" or consistent players who don't usually attack at all during the match are very successful a lot of times. They don't make very many errors and don't hit many winners either. They wait for you to make all the mistakes, which creates addition pressure on you.

SOLUTION:

"Pushers" usually need to be forced to make mistakes. One of the best ways to get them to make mistakes is by bringing them to the net with a drop shot or short ball and then simply making them volley or hit an overhead which is normally what they do worst since they spend so much time on the backcourt keeping the ball consistently in play. If you have a strong net game you should attack the net with fast, low shots forcing them to risk more by going for a passing shot or lob. Both strategies are effective against this style of play.

CHAPTER 2: STRATEGIES AGAINST ADVANCED STYLES OF PLAY

Strategy #8
What to do against a heavy topspin player

PROBLEM:

Heavy topspin is becoming more and more popular in today's game. It usually bounces up fast and high which makes it difficult to attack or come into the net. It will either force you to step back or move forward to hit the ball.

SOLUTION:

You can do several things to counter-attack heavy topspin balls. 1. You can simply step back and let the ball come down to a comfortable hitting position for you. This way you're not hitting at or above should height which is a much harder shot to hit for most people. 2. You can hit the ball as it's rising before it gets too high and step into the court as you do this. Doing this requires more skill then letting it come back down but it can be rewarding if you can keep your opponent rushed with you quick on-the-rise returns.

Strategy #9
How to overcome the slice-only player

PROBLEM:
Some tennis payers will only hit slice shots because they are either very successful doing this or because they don't know how to hit any other types of shots. The ball will stay low and short which makes it harder to attack or hit clean winners off.

SOLUTION:
Being patient with this type of player pays off in the long run. The key is not to over hit those low slices. Try to get low and move forward. The best way to get them to miss is by either, getting them on the run and then closing the net when they slice it back, or to mix up the heights on them. Mixing up heights basically means hitting a low topspin shot and then a high topspin shot and continuing to follow this pattern until they don't find the correct angle on their racquet forcing them to hit too low at the net or too high and out.

Strategy #10
How to return a big serve

PROBLEM:
Big servers are tough opponents because of the speed at which the ball comes at you. The ball will come hard and fast, without much warning.

SOLUTION:
Keep a short back swing and move your feet before the ball comes. Make to split-step when they are impacting the ball as to improve your reaction time. The secret to returning fast serves is not to over hit. Learn to use your opponent's power by simply returning a well-placed ball. A lot of times you will noticed that you don't need to hit the ball harder for it to be a good return and that's the most important thing to remember. Move your feet, keep your eyes on the ball, take a short back swing , and move forward as you hit the ball to have success with this shot.

Strategy #11
How to counter a drop shot

PROBLEM:
Drop shots are great weapons to have since they don't require any power. It's a finesse shot or also known as a touch shot. Drop shots are just as valuable as hitting a winner or an overhead. Remember that the distance going side to side on the court is shorter than the distance moving forward to the net. When you hit a drop shot you actually make your opponent run a longer distance.

SOLUTION:
The best counter shot against a drop shot is simply to hit another drop shot back. This way you have a lesser chance of getting passed or lobbed or even getting aimed at. If can master this shot, you will make more than one opponent struggle running forward for a shot they did not expect. The second shot you can hit against a drop shot is a deep return to your opponent's weaker side and then simply expect to hit a volley or overhead. If you want to reduce the amount of drop shots your opponent hit to you, you can either hit the ball hard and deep or keep the ball high and deep. This will make it a lot harder for them to hit a drop shot.

Strategy #12
How to overcome the runner

PROBLEM:
Runners are tough adversaries because they normally don't give up and they get many balls back in play. Some players win their matches with sheer speed. They chase ball after ball until their opponents end up going for too much and finally miss.

SOLUTION:
Runners always have a weaker shot. It could be their backhand, forehand, serve, volleys, or overhead. Find their weakest shot and start attacking that shot instead of going for winners. You have to understand that their biggest strength is their speed so you have to focus on what they do worst even though that means not hitting clean winners. You have to be patient and allow them to make the mistakes with their weakest shot. Insist and be persistent until they start making errors with that shot and then don't deviate from the plan. You'll be tempted to finish the point but it always pays to stick with the plan instead of allowing your opponent to do what they do best, which is run down balls. To beat these types of players attack their weaknesses, not their speed since that's where you will end up working the hardest to win points. Stick with the plan and be persistent.

Strategy #13
How to out-play a big forehand

PROBLEM:

Big or power forehands are common in tennis as everyone has to have weapons in order to win points and more often than not, their forehands are their strongest shots. In today's game power forehands have become a necessity to win more points as players get faster and stronger which means the ball needs to go faster and harder if you want to get past them.

SOLUTION:

Big forehands are big as long as they are being hit in their power zones, which is normally between the knees and shoulder height. If you can make them hit shots below the height of their knees and above the height of their shoulders, chances are their forehands won't be as big any more. Try hitting low slices to their forehand or high topspin to reduce the amount of power they can generate off that side.

**Strategy #14
How to overcome a big hitter**

PROBLEM:

Big hitters overpower their opponents off both wings and can often start points with a blazing serve. They win points by simply hitting harder than others.

SOLUTION:

You need to slow down big hitters with some off-speed shots like: slow slices, side-slices, high topspin, deep balls, drop shots and short angles. Big hitters hate changes in ball speeds because it forces them to have to adjust to the depth, height and speed the ball. After a while these changes in speed, spin, and height make big hitters either miss or have to slow down to reduce their errors. That when you know you got them out of their game plan and now you can start winning more points.

CHAPTER 3: STRATEGIES AGAINST UNSUAL STYLES OF PLAY

Strategy #15
How to beat the "grunter"

PROBLEM:

The "grunter" can be loud and distracting. They will grunt every time they hit the ball and will increase the loudness of the grunt depending on the length of the point, importance of the point, or on how tired they are.

SOLUTION:

Learn to focus on the more important aspects of your game like breathing and footwork. Focusing too much on what your opponent is doing will distract you and keep you away from playing your best tennis. Find things that you can focus on in between point like: fixing your strings, tying your shoe strings if they are untied or loose, toweling off when you're sweaty. If it's too much distraction for you, simply grunt as well.

Strategy #16
How to beat the time-delaying player

PROBLEM:
Players who intentional delay time between points and change-overs are looking to control the tempo of the match. Some players need to play fast in order to maintain them tempo while others don't mind playing slower. Slowing down a match when you're losing is a great strategy as it gives you more time to fix any mistakes your making and get back on track. When someone does this to you it can be difficult to find your game again.

SOLUTION:
Focus on what you need to be doing. Don't fall into their trap by delaying the match. Simply stand ready every time and show them that you are ready to go.

Strategy #17
How to overcome a fast paced player

PROBLEM:
Some players like to rush through points, not allowing their opponents to take their time and think things through which causes more errors if you're not used to being rushed. They usually take short water breaks and are always starting to serve before you get to the baseline to return serve.

SOLUTION:
When someone is constantly rushing play, the best plan is to simply slow things down to where you feel comfortable and know you won't make errors due to being rushed.

Some of the best ways to accomplish this are:

- Toweling off, drinking water and breathing slowly during change-overs.
- Putting your towel on the back or side fence in between points as to have to walk to dry off with your towel and slow down play.
- Tying your shoe strings before serving or before returning serve.
- Fixing your racquet strings before serving or before returning serve.

Strategy #18
How to beat the crowd favorite

PROBLEM:
Crowd favorite players can have quite a following during points. Some crowds and family members can very loud and intense which makes it hard for anyone to focus on the match. They clap when you lose a point. They clap on important points and in the middle of rallies.

SOLUTION:
Crowd favorites are difficult opponents when they are winning but when they are losing things get quite. Concentrate on beginning the match winning and stay on top. The bigger the lead you have, the less noise you will hear from the crowd. Some of their fans, family members, and other people will simply leave the match which will mean less distraction for you and better results. If you're the type of player that actually enjoys having a crowd against you while competing, then I would still recommend that you start winning and continue to stay on top until the match is over. Crowd favorites are only favorites while they are winning or at least have a chance at winning but if you can prove they have no chance, and then you will have a much easier time.

Strategy #19
How to counter soft angles

PROBLEM:

Soft angles are great weapons to have because they force players to step off the baseline and into the front and side court. This opens up the entire court for your opponent and practically allows them to have almost full control of the point.

SOLUTION:

The best way to counter a soft angled shot is to do one of three things:

- Follow the ball to the net and cut off the angle that was just created.
- Return another angle crosscourt and step back into the middle of the court.
- Hit a drop shot right in front of you as to bring your opponent to the net and then cover the middle of the court to block any possibility of a passing shot.

Strategy #20
How to counter deep and high shots

PROBLEM:
Deep high shots, if done consistently, will cause many errors from most tennis players. They basically push you far back behind the baseline and they force you to hit falling back which reduces the amount of power you can generate on your next shot. Even they are done with or without topspin; they still represent a threat and require a good counter-attack.

SOLUTION:

Deep high shots can be countered in a number of ways:

- You can step back and return another high deep shot and how your opponent reacts to this shot.
- You can hit it on the rise as soon as the ball bounces.
- You can slice the ball back to keep the ball low and short.

Besides countering their high deep shots, you can also prevent them from hitting this type of shot by:

- Hitting low angled slice or topspin strokes.
- Catching the ball in the air by hitting a volley or swinging volley to keep the ball from landing deep.
- Slicing low short shots that force your opponent to step into the court and make it much more difficult for them to hit another accurate high deep shot.

**Strategy #21
How to overcome high backhands**

PROBLEM:

High backhands are one of the most troublesome shots for most players, especially if you have a one-handed backhand. High backhands require more strength to bring back into the court and backhands normally are not the ones to hit the best high shots with.

SOLUTION:

You can overcome high backhands in three ways:

1. You can run around your backhand and hit a forehand.
2. You can hit your backhand on the rise before it becomes a high backhand.
3. You can step back as far as necessary as to hit a mid-height or low backhand again.

Strategy #22
How to beat the scrap-shot player

PROBLEM:
Scrap-shot players hit unorthodox balls with tricky spins and normally not very good technique but they get the ball in and don't make it easy to attack their shots. Some of the shots they usually hit are: slice, side-slice, side-topspin, moon balls, and drop shots that bounce and return to the net and soft touch shots.

SOLUTION:
When you don't know what to expect, the best solution is to stay on your toes and be prepared to hit all types of shots. Make sure you get close to the ball as it will move around more than usual. If you're not comfortable with the way the ball is bounce, attack the net where you will be hitting the ball in the air and not have to worry about how the ball bounces.

CHAPTER 4: MENTAL STRATEGIES

Strategy #23
How to overcome nerves

PROBLEM:
Getting nervous during a tennis match is a natural reaction. The important thing is not letting your nerves get in the way of your performance. Sometimes being too nervous make you freeze during important points which force you to make silly mistakes or to increase your chances of missing.

SOLUTION:
There are a number of ways to overcome nerves.

 Here are just a few that work very well for most tennis players:

-       Move your feet. A lot of times when you get nervous, you stop moving your feet which increases errors. Moving your feet more and quicker will help you to meet the ball better and will relax you during the point.
-       Breathe during the point in and out. In as the balls comes to you and out as you impact the ball. When you not playing the point it's even more important to breathe deeply to relax your muscles and help you focus on your strategy instead of what you're feeling.
-       Lowering your intensity level. Try thinking positively about what you are planning to do during the point and breathing deeply and slowly to lower your heart rate.

Strategy #24
How to overcome stress in a match

PROBLEM:
Stress is another natural factor that occurs when you feel strained and under pressure to perform or by outside forces such as family, friends, being late, forgetting tennis equipment, weather conditions, etc.

SOLUTION:
To overcome stress you have to understand what is causes the stress in the first place. If you late to your match, you should make sure to take your time and not rush. You won't make up for lost time by going faster. That will actually promote more missed shots than anything else. If you're stressed about the weather and feel that it might start raining, you should focus on one point at a time and let the weather do what it will do regardless of what's going on in the match. If it's a family member, that's causing the stress, you should try to focus your attention on your match and block them from your mind if they are affecting your negatively. You can also ask them to please stay quiet during the match or to simply leave and come back after the match is done. Family members want you to be successful but the stress of the match can be too much for them. Focus on what is causing the stress and solve it so that you can focus on winning.

**Strategy #25
How to stay focused until the end**

PROBLEM:

Stay focused in your match until it's over is not an easy task since it requires hard work. Some people start good but finish terribly because of a lack of focus. Others never focus long enough to close a game or a set.

SOLUTION:

Staying focused during the entire match requires a few things.

1. You need to have visual reminders that will help you to keep your mind on what's most important to you in the match or what is helping you win more points. One of the best ways to do this is to have notes written down on a piece of paper that you can glance at during change-overs. This way you keep remembering what you need to be doing.

2. Write down on a sticker two or three important things that will help you stay focused in your match and place the sticker on a safe place on your racquet where it won't fall off. The inside of the neck of a tennis racquet is a great place to put a sticker. The neck of a tennis racquet is located between the grip and the strings.

**Strategy #26
What to think during change-
overs**

PROBLEM:
Change-overs are one of the most underestimated times to think during a tennis match. What should you be thinking? You're tired and thirsty so why should you be thinking about anything? Well, change-overs are the best time to do what is most important in tennis and that is to think in order to find solutions to problems you're having in the match and finally succeed.

SOLUTION:
During change-overs you should be thinking about what is making you win points and what is making you lose points. If you're not winning points you should figure out why that is.

Maybe your opponent is taking control of the point from the start and forcing you to hit backhands only and not allowing you to use your forehand which might be your winning shot.

Maybe you're not moving your feet enough and need to start focusing on that.

Maybe your tired and want to win faster but don't know how but during the change-over you realize you need to be more aggressive and possible attack the net more or hit more drop shots.

Maybe your opponent isn't doing anything special and you're the one making all the errors. You realize this during the change-over and decide you need to start keeping the ball in play longer or force your opponent to make more mistakes.

**Strategy #27
What to think before a match**

PROBLEM:

Before the match it's important to think things through as to prepare a plan of attack but knowing what to think makes a big difference when it comes to winning and losing.

SOLUTION:

Yes, during the match you should do your best not to think too much but before the match you should definitely be preparing what you will be doing during the match so that you can go on "auto-pilot" during the match and simply execute what you thought of beforehand. You should be thinking about what you need to be doing be most successful.
This could include:

- Moving your feet.
- Tossing the ball high on your serve.
- Following through on your ground strokes.
- Keep your eyes on the ball.
- Not rushing during points.
- To attack your opponents weakness right from the start.
- Attack your opponents' second serve.
- Not to let surroundings distract you.

**Strategy #28
What to think the night before a match**

PROBLEM:

The night before the match you should rest and think only about things you will have control over. Don't worry about things that won't benefit you in any way like rain, wind, etc. Make sure your body and mind rest the night before the match as you don't want to begin a new day tired or weak.

SOLUTION:

The night before the match you should practice visualizing how you would like to play the following day.

You can imagine specific strategies you'd like to perform such as:

- Slicing and attacking the net.
- Hitting high topspin shots to your opponents backhand or weaker side.
- Having long rallies crosscourt.

Other things you could be visualizing the night before could be:

- Seeing you chase down difficult shots from corner to corner.
- Standing confident to return serve.
- Tossing the ball proudly before serving.
- Being motivated and energetic in between points.

**Strategy #29
What to do when you're a set down**

PROBLEM:
When you're a set down you start doubting yourself and begin feeling you won't win the match. Know what to do to change things around is both emotional and physical.

SOLUTION:
When you are down a set you need to understand that the key is in knowing where it is that you're losing points and winning points.

If you're missing a lot of high shots and that's what your opponent if forcing you to hit most of the time, then you should try attacking the net more and reduce the amount of high shots you hit from the back court.

If you're losing long rallies because your fitness level isn't as strong as your opponents, then you should figure out a way to key points short. You could bring your opponent to the net more often or go for more winners.

If you're winning points when you run around your backhand and hit forehands, then you should try to run around as many shots and hit forehands.

If you won all the points where you made your first serve in, then you should focus on going for more first serves.

Strategy #30
What to do when you are a set up

PROBLEM:

If you won the first set, you have an emotional and psychological edge over in the match which weighs heavily. What should you do in the second set to win the match?

SOLUTION:

After winning the first set you know your opponent will make a greater effort to get on top in the score. Also, you know you're close to the finish line since you've already finished have the race.

The key is to do these 3 things:

1.   Keep doing what you're doing to win points. Changing a winning strategy is not the right plan at this point. Don't make foolish changes by being less aggressive or more aggressive.

2.   Make an extra effort for the first 3 games of the match so that you start with very good lead. This will demoralize your opponent and make the remainder of the match easier. 3-0 or 2-0 or 4-0 are all great starts to a second set.

3.   Make sure you stay on top in the score until the match ends as to not let your opponent even consider they have a chance at winning the match because if you don't do this, you will definitely regret it later on.

**Strategy #31
What to do when you have match point**

PROBLEM:

Match point can viewed in many different ways. Having the right approach makes all the difference. Being overconfident or doubting yourself are both very common but negative reactions to a match point. What you should you do?

SOLUTION:

Match point is the greatest opportunity in a match to win. Make sure you don't think too much during match point. Keep things simple. Whatever is making you win should be repeated during match point without a doubt and done with precision. If you get nervous, simply breathe and move your feet to get rid of some of the nerves. Don't look around or let yourself get distracted.

Remember:

STICK WITH THE ORIGINAL PLAN!

Strategy #32
What to do after serving a double fault

PROBLEM:

Double faults affect you emotionally and psychologically. They are normal and can happen to you during a match as long as you don't do them too often. The difference is in what you do and think after you double fault to correct the situation.

SOLUTION:

Focus on what you need to do to get your serve in. Second serves require a higher degree of control because it's your last chance to get your serve in. Don't add any pressure to yourself or get nervous.

Make sure your follow these 5 steps to double fault less:

1. Be selective with your tosses. Don't hit every toss. Take your time and only hit serves you feel will have a high chance of going in due to a well-placed toss.
2. Don't rush with your service motion.
3. Bounce the ball at least 4 times before serving as to slow you down.
4. Following through on your swing.
5. Keep your chin and head up when you impact the ball so that you can keep your eyes on the ball as long as possible.

CHAPTER 5: MENTAL TACTICS

33. "Know thy opponent"

Knowing whom you are going to be up against before the match begins is extremely important. They have probably already done their homework and know more about you than you can imagine. If this is so you should go around and ask about the player you are going to be up against. You can ask friends, past opponents, team mates, anybody that can give information regarding your opponent. This information is only useful to you before the match starts, after that you will probably learn the rest on the court. Even if your opponent isn't scouting you, do your homework on him or her.

There are two main reasons why it is beneficial to scout your opponent: The first one is because you will be able to analyze his/her strengths and weaknesses. When you know this, you can decide what strategy will work best in the match. The second reason is because you will have time to rehearse the match in your mind before you even enter the tennis court. Another word also used for this kind of mental practice is "visualization". You can practice the strokes and strategies you want to use, in your mind and not get physically get tired.

High performance tennis depends greatly on this practice. Many people daydream about their match and how they are going to play and don't realize they are visualizing their game. Most of us have done it at one time or another. When you know how your opponent plays, what they like and don't like to do, their mental and physical capabilities, you can generate an accurate game plan. Mental capabilities means just how strong the mental aspect of their game is.. Physical capabilities means how well prepared they are to physically compete. Maybe your opponent is scouting you and knows how s/he will play you. He has the edge and you don't want this. The best thing you can do before a match starts is be prepared. Know your opponent.

34. "The match ends, when it ends"

Matches often become contests where both players are waiting to see which one will give in first. Luckily for you a match can be won even if your one point away from losing. Many people have won after being down 6/0 6/0 0-40 deficit. This is what makes tennis so competitive. You have to be concentrated until the end of the match.

Confidence has a big role in competition, since a weak mental competitor may be ahead in a match and then lose it. Other times s/he may be down in the match and not make an effort to come back or at least give a good fight. Many players have learned not to let past circumstances affect their future matches in a negative manner. A good competitor will fight to the very end because s/he can come back and win the match despite the score. Other good competitors know how not to let an opponent back into the match and finally finish them off. Finishing a match and coming back from a deficit are some of the hardest things to accomplish in any level of play. Make sure to remind yourself that "the match ends, when it ends" so that you may become a competitor feared by others and remembered for your persistence.

APPLICATION
Practice playing from 5-0 or 4-0 up in each set and then try to finish the match. As soon as you finish your first match alternate with your practice partner as soon as you finish the first match. You should play many sets to get used to this mentality.

35. "Prepare for success"

Success comes to those who are prepared for it. As in life this should be your mentality on the tennis court. Some players just put on some clothes, sun block, take some balls and a racquet, and head for the court. There they hit a couple of balls and say "serves up". Many people have only a few minutes to prepare for a practice session or match and their behavior would appear quite reasonable for the short time span available to them.

Now, let's take another approach to preparation. First make a list of equipment needs and check off all the things you carry out on to the court. When you have what you physically need get mentally prepared for competition. Finally get a good warm up. This is just a general outline of a basic preparation plan. Now let's look at a specific one. These are all the basic things you will require on the court before you enter.

These are just a few. You can add more if you would like. Some of these things might seem silly but you never know how silly you will feel when you don't have them and desperately need them. Prevent from having bad moments, by having the right tools for the job. Don't be too proud to ask somebody help, even your opponent. We have all been in those painful situations and know how it feels. Most of us will gladly help each other out.

Now that you have you have your equipment ready, get your mind on the task at hand. Some people like to visualize, others get energized or pumped by talking to themselves, and many listen to music to relax. Some like to watch tennis on TV or on the court. Everybody has a different approach to get ready for a match. Sample these and other approaches to see what gets you best, mentally prepared. This is a very important part in preparation for a match. Don't take it lightly.

If you want to play tennis for many years, get a good warm up before every practice and match. You can't imagine the benefits of warming up correctly.

Start with some light stretching, this will get your muscles to become elastic. Then jog for a few minutes. You can jog in the same place or around a certain area, as long as you get your body warmed up. After this, do some mini-tennis and gradually distance yourself from the net until you get to the backcourt where you can slowly increase the speed of the ball.

36. "Keep a poker face"

Most people would agree that some of the best poker players in the world are those who can keep the same face when dealt good or bad cards. This might seem strange for some to believe but it's especially true in tennis. Have you noticed how the hardest players to beat keep a straight face and show hardly and emotions or change in their gestures? This can be frustrating for people who like to see their opponents whine and throw their racquets when they perform poorly or when they lose a crucial point. Poker face players are tough competitors because they don't transmit their true feelings while on the court. Even when desperate to win, they prefer to show that necessity through concentration and calmness. Don't think they don't have emotions. They are just hidden for the moment. Try this approach to become a better competitor. Maybe you perform better when you show your emotions and that's great, but for anybody who wants to try something new, this is a good start. It can change the way you view tennis and you will start to see things you never saw before that were always present. Great things can happen when you concentrate and focus on the task at hand. When you are calm and emotionless, you greatly enhance your concentration. Keep a poker face when you play to see who is bluffing and who really has what it takes to win.

37. "Hide your weaknesses, exploit theirs"

Ever notice how some players seem to be perfect on the court? Why hasn't anybody broken their game? Maybe they are very good at hiding things from others. Things they don't want you to know, like a weakness? If you don't know their weakness, where are you going to attack them? In a match, a player is at a disadvantage when s/he does not know an opponents weakness.

Before the match starts, find out what your opponent's weakness is and figure out how you can exploit it. Ask other players and friends if they know this person. You can even look on the Internet under the players name and see what helpful information is out there for you. If nobody knows this person, find out for yourself in the warm up. Hit some to their forehand, then their backhand. After that, mix up the height and spin of the ball. You will eventually find something they do poorer than the rest of their game.

For example, when you have a weak backhand, learn to run around it and hit a forehand. Another example could be if your weakness is your bad physical fitness and don't want long rallies from the baseline. In this case it is better to attack the net or keep the points short. This way your hiding your weaknesses and exploiting theirs.

APPLICATION
Have your practice partner attack your weakness with his/her weapon. At first it will feel awkward, but this will help you overcome these situations in a match. Then, have your partner hit with his/her weaker side and you with your weapon (you are simply doing the opposite). This will give a better understanding of how skillful your weapon really is and how much improvement is needed. You are learning to play defense and offense.

38. "He who gets the last ball in, wins"

There are many philosophies as to how tennis should be played. The simplest possible one is "who ever gets the last ball in, wins". When the ball goes to the net or outside the singles lines, you lose the point. And when you keep the ball in, you win. This might seem very elemental, but some of the hardest things to accomplish are sometimes the elemental ones.

APPLICATION

To achieve this law, practice consistency. Get 10 balls consistently over the net and in. When you have completed 10, strive for 20. Decide what your goal will be and strive to obtain it. For example, my goal for this month is to get at least 100 balls over with my partner. When this has been achieved you can start being specific with the area, height and spin with which you hit. This will be specified in more detail in law #24.

39. "Be true to thy self"

In close matches, we all get the urge to call a ball out when it is near the line. Have you heard of the saying "when in doubt, call it out"? This of course is not ethical or correct. Don't let the pressure of the moment make you be an unjust player. If it's a close call and you are not sure about it, repeat the point. It's the right thing to do. You save a lot of time and some heated arguments. Be true to yourself. Call the ball as you see it. You will feel a lot better about yourself and be respected by others.

APPLICATION
Watch a practice live match and try to call the ball in or out in your head, not out loud. This way you will practice calling close shots more often even when you are not playing. After a while you will instinctively know if a ball was good or bad.

40. "He who hits first, hits twice"

Whenever you attack in a point you will be in command and will have better options to finish off the point. In other words, when you start attacking you will be able to continue to be offensive (most of the time). Don't wait for things to happen. Go out there and do your best to be the one who is in charge of the point. Learn to be proactive and not reactive. A proactive person acts in advance to deal with an expected difficulty. A reactive person responds to a stimulus. In tennis reacting to things that happen on the court is normal. When you learn to be proactive, your chances of winning increase many times over. Take control of the point. Hit first so that you may hit twice.

41. "Be a fake to win"

Many people feel that they don't have the confidence or courage to win a match in pressure situations. Why not become an actor on the tennis court and play the role of the confident or courageous tennis player. Be a fake and you'll win more often than you think. Choose the way you want to be seen on and off the court. Then act like that person you want to be. You will feel a bit awkward at first, but you will get used to it with some practice. Some people don't understand the importance of the image you exert on the court.

An example of this could be if you have just played a very long first set and you are very tired. Your opponent also looks tired, but you decide to carry yourself in an energetic and positive manner. Make them think you can do this for another two sets. This can be very demoralizing for anyone. They will take one look at you and notice they have no chance (even though both of you feel just as tired inside). Your opponent decides that s/he can't handle a second set with somebody who seems not to get tired and chooses to forfeit. How about that! This does not always happen. Being a fake will surely improve your chances of winning. All actors work very hard to perfect their image. They know their success depends on it. Maybe you won't win an "Oscar" for your performance, but you'll win many more matches.

42. "Bring down the walls"

Every tennis player has his/her own castle to protect. Its walls keep enemies from breaking in. But if those walls are brought down, there is very little hope for that castle. Some tennis players walls are their serve or their forehand. Others have speed or patience as their walls. When you break don a players wall you have an open gate towards attacking weaker shots. Learn to "bring down the walls" and you'll win many battles.

APPLICATION

Have your practice partner be the aggressive player and you play defensively. In other words, your practice partner will attack and try to finish the point while you just keep the ball in play waiting for him/her to miss. Once both of you get the hang of it, switch. Now you become the aggressive player and s/he becomes the defensive player. This way you will learn to bring down those walls and advance to weaker territory. Remember you are working towards disarming their weapons on way or another.

43. "Learn from every match"

Mistakes are justified when you learn from them and correct them. Don't get into the habit of making unforced errors and never learning from them. This will hurt you in competitive match situations. The best way to view unforced errors is as a learning process that will take time and dedication. Keep fixing and correcting them throughout your practices and matches and watch your tennis level go up sky high. Every match tells us something. It's a waking moment. We must open our eyes and see what we need to see. So much knowledge can be accumulated through experience. Keep a log of all your experiences so that you may grow by their knowledge. Try using this sample "after match log":

AFTER MATCH LOG
DATE:
OPPONENT:
TOURNAMENT:
RATE YOURSELF FROM 1-10:
(10 BEING YOUR BEST PERFORMANCE)

WHAT I DID RIGHT IN THE MATCH

WHAT I DID WRONG IN THE MATCH

WHAT I LEARNED

WHAT I WILL DO TO APPLY WHAT I HAVE LEARNED

Many times we don't learn from mistakes because we are not reminded of them. Remind yourself of all the little things you need to do to keep improving and obtaining your goals. Look through your "after match logs" at least once a weak.

44. "Acquire knowledge"

Tennis Ball + Racquet + Knowledge = Success

Don't be too proud to ask for help. Many tennis instructors will be glad to help you if you ask them to. Keep in mind that some are more specialized in certain areas than others. Know what you want to improve or learn and have them help you. You'll save a lot of time learning from their errors, than by making your own errors and having to learn from them. Information on all different topics is available in tennis books, magazines, videos and on the Internet.

The more you know the more creative you can be with your tennis. You will be much better at making decisions when you have more information to decide on.

45. "Know thy rules"

It's very useful to know what the rules of tennis are. Some people don't realize how many advantages can be obtained from having knowledge about:
Court dimensions
Singles rules
Doubles rules
Mixed doubles rules
Racquets
Balls
The let
Order of serve
Coaching
Wheelchair tennis rules

DID YOU KNOW?

Did you know the net is lower over the center of the court? And did you know that when you play crosscourt, you are actually hitting a high percentage shot (A shot that will have a higher percentage of going in than if you go down the line.) since the distance crosscourt is greater than the distance down the line? As you can see, the rules of tennis can be very helpful when you want to play wiser and more efficient.

APPLICATION
Obtain a copy of your tennis associations' rulebook and look over it to see how many new things you learned from it. Look at the section on the amount of time you have between points, games, sets and matches. Then take advantage of this knowledge. Practice timing yourself between points and changeovers so that you may become accustomed to the short time periods you will have in competition. Also practice playing points and then

giving yourself no more then 30 seconds of rest. Work on your physical conditioning. This will help you to keep up with the rhythm you desire to maintain in a match.

46. "Build your chess board"

Tennis is like a chessboard; you have to put the pieces in the all right places. When you position yourself in the right place at the right time, you find yourself hitting the ideal shot. Things don't just happen you have to make them happen. Be ready to improvise.

APPLICATION

First, work on having all the basic strokes. When you have accomplished doing this, mix different shots and strokes in different situations. This will help you build your game plan for each match

Practice #1

Alternate hitting topspin and backspin (slice) with your forehand. Try not to repeat the same spin twice. Only your hitting partner can hit with the same spin pattern. When you can do this well on the forehand side, do the same with the backhand. You alternate spins and your partner hits with the same spin. Then switch with your partner.

Practice #2

One player hits crosscourt while the other player hits down the line (straight). The pattern made by the strokes has the shape of an eight (8). When you are done practicing, change the patterns between you and your partner.

47. "Find the pattern"

Many players are taught to play tennis in a way that can often be predictable. They learn to hit the ball to a certain place over and over. They are also taught to do certain things in specific points such as match point or set point. If you learn what their pattern is, you can predict what they will do. When you learn how to decipher a person's pattern they won't be able to surprise you. Their game will be vulnerable once you know where the ball is going and what you will do to take advantage of this situation.

You don't need to be a mathematician to learn to find patterns. Watch some tennis matches in your neighborhood or on TV. Try to find different patterns of play in each point, game, set, or even in the entire match.

Some examples of patterns are:

      Crosscourt pattern   Down-the-line pattern

* Remember that every player has his or her own pattern. Some are simpler and others are more complex.

48. "Pawn check mates king"

In chess, you will often find yourself in situations where you must use your weakest pieces to win. In tennis this happens often. It's very hard to wake up everyday and play your best. Once in a while, you will play a match when your tennis is not at its best and that's when it counts the most to bring out the champion in you. Winning when your are performing at lower level of tennis than your used to is quite a challenge, but this is where you separate yourself from the rest. Be victorious in the best and worst of times.

APPLICATION

Play a match where your practice partner attacks your weakness with his/her weapon. Do this for no more than forty-five minutes and then switch. After both of you have completed at least two sets, play some practice points in which you can hit anywhere you like and see how comfortable you now feel when you have to come up with big shots with your weaker side.

Play a competitive match with someone other than your practice partner. Compare your performance to that of past matches where your weakness was the cause of your loss. You will notice that you have a lot more confidence in your weaker side then before. This will help you win tough matches even when you are not playing your best. There are other techniques that can be used for different circumstances, but this is a good start.

49. "Build a base"

In life, we usually have different plans for the same objectives. We have plan A and if plan A doesn't get the job done, we use plan B. When plan B can't get the job done, we use plan C. This is called building a strategic base. In tennis you might have to change your game plans many times in a single match. It is wise to have a base strategy or a strategy, which we think is best, suited for the opponent you are up against. Build a base and when you have done this, think of alternative strategies that can be used if anything goes wrong.

Obviously, you will have plan A that is your best game strategy or the game your most comfortable with. Now you need to decide what is going to be your plan B. If your plan A is based on pounding winners from the baseline, your plan B could be attacking the net. That way you speed up the rhythm of play. Finally, plan C might just be keeping the ball in play and waiting for your opponent to make the errors. This will slow down your rhythm of play.

If something doesn't work for you, try going from your plan A to plan B. If plan B is not the solution, try plan C. Always have at least three alternative strategies you can fall back on, but first build a base. Your base is the plan with which you start every match. It is usually the one that has given you the best results in the past and which you feel most comfortable with.

50. "Don't dry up the well"

The most logical way to win is through the use of your weapon/s. But when you use a weapon much too often your opponent becomes accustomed to it. This becomes dangerous for you. It's good to keep opponents guessing. Use your weapon as much as possible but mix up some other shots to keep them off balance. Don't let them get used to seeing the same pattern or the same stroke much too often. Don't dry up the well. Become unpredictable.

APPLICATION
A good way to learn or improve the way you mix up your shots is by being specific in your practice. Play some points with your practice partner where neither of you are not allowed to hit the same shot twice. At first, do this without serving. Just start the point with an underhand toss. An example of this drill could be:

Hit a forehand:

With topspin
With slice
Flat
Deep into the court with topspin
Short into the court with topspin
Deep into the court with slice
Short into the court with slice

Hit a backhand:

With topspin
With slice
Flat
Deep into the court with topspin
Short into the court with topspin

Deep into the court with slice
Short into the court with slice

NOTE: Shots can be repeated as long as they are alternated with another stroke. You can make it as simple as you want. When you become skillful you can add as many different shots as you want. It is best to start mixing two or three different shots and gradually add more with time.

51. "Mind over matter"

Tennis starts as a physical game but then transcends into a more mental game. Things that our physical body can't do, our mind can do many times over. The power of the mind is unimaginable. Emotions and thoughts become extremely important when we get nervous or uncomfortable in competition. Our body will do things we sometimes wonder. "Why didn't I just lift my arm a little higher and get the ball over the net?" What we have to remember is that our mind controls our body and it is just doing what our mind has told it to do. Work on controlling your emotions. They can become great allies in times of need. Concentration is basic in competition. It is a great skill that can be learned with some practice. It is one of the hardest things to master, but very valuable indeed.

52. "Only give presents on birthdays"

Most of us know how important it is not to give up any points in a match and especially when it is a close one. We often give away some presents that eventually hurt us in the long run. Minimize those presents or unforced errors when competing. Only give presents on birthdays.

APPLICATION

An excellent way to minimize presents is by improving your consistency. The next time you step on the tennis court after you've warmed up, take just one ball out and keep that ball in play with your practice partner for as long as possible. You want to accustom yourself to keep the ball in play right from the first point. When you practice this, count how many times you get the ball in without missing. When you have missed that first ball after maintaining it in play for a while, choose a specific side, stroke and spin with which you want to hit and do the same consistency exercise. For example: Hit crosscourt forehands with topspin. Try to keep the ball in play for as long as possible without missing and then write down the amount of times the ball went in. Do this for each side you practice (forehand and backhand) and compare it with your next days practice. You should at least do this with these exercises: crosscourt forehands, crosscourt backhands, forehand backhand down the line and backhand forehand down the line.

53. "Have the heart of a lion"

Tennis matches and tournaments are won in many ways. Some are won, by having an extraordinary skill. Others are won, by being in better physical condition than the rest. The way specified in this law is probably the most important and least paid attention to HEART. It has the power to bring our level of tennis to a perfect ten. It can make you become feared amongst competitors. Most important of all, it will make you victorious.

54. "Choose your weapon"

When you start to improve your level of tennis, you will feel more in control. This control is the beginning of your specialization. Everybody has something they do better than the rest. This is what allows you to control the point through one or all of these: power, placement, spin, and consistency. This is called your "weapon". The more you improve your weapon, the more dangerous you'll become. Some players have unpredictable serves. Others have powerful forehands or backhands. Many win with their speed and athleticism. Find your weapon and when you do, enhance it's potential by creating another weapon. That way you'll have two weapons and become a double threat for others.

55. "Perfection by imitation"

Some of the greatest artists of all time began by imitating their favorite painters and then went on to create their own style and form of art. Creating your own style of play is also a wonderful thing to do but this might take some time. Tennis can also be imitated and then perfected. Look for a specific professional tennis player who has the style of play you desire. Then read about him/her. Watch their matches on TV. Try to mimic their every detail, until you master their style of play. When you do, make it your own by adjusting it until you feel comfortable. Remember, don't become a copy of another tennis player, just take what they do best and make it better.

56. "The four leaf clover"

Four-leaf clovers, a lucky rabbit's foot, horseshoes are all forms of good luck charms and they all bring you good luck. Is luck important in tennis? Yes. Why? Well, because there are just things that we cannot control no matter what we do. Can we let luck be the deciding factor in the result of our match? No. We must improve our chances by doing the right things like: prepare correctly for a match, analyze opponents, use adequate strategies, be positive and stay focused. These are just a few, but it's a beginning. Luck comes to those who look for it. Don't wait for the right moment or the right match to play your true potential. Do it right now. Start with the very first point and continue until the end of the match. You will know which matches or points are the result of luck. Those points didn't come without a little hard work.

APPLICATION:
Make your own luck and see the results. The best way to make your own luck is through goal setting. Choose goals that can be measured. That way you can see your improvement and decide if changes need to be made to your goals. Once you know what these goals are decide how you are going to achieve them and write it down. Then, make daily goals that will help you achieve your main goals.

Write down your daily goals on an index card and carry it everywhere you go. Every time your about to do something ask yourself: "Is this getting me closer to my goal?" If it isn't, then stop doing it. If it is, then your on your way to success.

This is a simple example:
Your goal may be: "improve my first serve percentage by

20%."
Now decide what you need to do to make this reality:

Have an expert take a look at my serve.
Practice "X" amount of serves per week.
Put more spin on the ball.
Improve my acceleration.
Increase leg strength.
Use targets in my practice (cones, balls, etc)

Now turn these ideas into daily goals and write them down on an index card so that you can check them many times a day.

57. "Humor for the brave"

When you are in tight matches and things aren't going the way you would like them to, you tend to get cranky, negative and careless. How do some players use these moments to make themselves stronger? Most of the careless mistakes you make in important points occur because of the pressure that you feel. A great way to get rid of that pressure is through humor. Whenever you make a silly mistake laugh at it. You can't imagine how relaxed you'll feel and how this can positively affect your game. When you are in a good mood, most things tend to go the way you want them to. Yes, you still want to win and still feel the pressure, but smiling or laughing at these mistakes can keep you competitive. When you are competitive you fight till the end and everyone can feel it. Don't take the easy way out yelling and throwing your racket. You'll enjoy tennis more if you laugh at the bad moments and continue to the good ones.

58. "Go where the party is at"

When you feel that practicing with your tennis partners or at a certain training facility is just not good enough anymore find an alternative. If you are not improving your level of play the way you'd like to or simply want to start competing on a regular basis, go where the party is. In other words, go where you can train the way you would like to or go where you may compete with whom you want. If you keep doing the same things, you'll keep getting the same results. It's up to you. What do you want to do with your tennis? Go where you need to be.

59. "Baby steps for giants"

True champions know that it takes time to become great. It all starts with those few steps and continues with more small steps, not leaps. Everything you do will seem effortless when you take your time. First you learn how to drive at 10mph. Then you learn to go a bit faster say 25mph. Later you go to 50mph. Finally after successive baby steps, you get to 100mph. The same thing applies in tennis. Don't get frustrated with slow improvements as long as they are gradual. These small improvements are the seed for future growth. Want to become a tennis giant? Then take baby steps to success.

60. "Thy second serve: may it serve you well"

The second serve can make you or break you as a tennis player. A good second serve will get you some easy points or at least put you in a good position to start the point. A bad second serve will make you double fault often and will permit your opponent to control the point right from the start. Practice these useful drills to increase your second serve percentage.

CHAPTER 6: FED DRILLS

Hitting over the rope cross court forehand

In this drill you will have to hit forehands over the rope crosscourt with top spin or flat balls that are fed to you by someone else on the other side of the net. Make sure you work on depth and control.

Hitting over the rope cross court backhand

In this drill you will have to hit backhands over the rope crosscourt with top spin or flat balls that are fed to you by someone else on the other side of the net. Make sure you work on depth and control.

Hitting over the rope down the line forehand

For this drill you should hit over the rope with top spin with your forehand down the line and have the ball land deep on the court. Make sure to focus on your follow through and to use your legs to generate spin. This can be a great offensive shot if your opponent has a weak backhand or has trouble with mid height balls or even high balls. Flat shots are allowed but this drill is most effectively done with top spin.

Hitting over the rope down the line backhand

For this drill you should hit over the rope with top spin with your backhand down the line and have the ball land deep on the court. Make sure to focus on your follow through and to use your legs to generate spin. This can be a great offensive shot if your opponent is attacking you backhand and you need to get them on the run with a safe shot. Flat shots are allowed but this drill is most effectively done with top spin.

Hitting over the rope alternating forehand and backhand cross court

For this drill you should hit over the rope with top spin with your forehand cross court and then the following shot with your backhand cross court. Continue doing this for the remainder of the drill. Work on keeping the ball deep on the court. Make sure to focus on your follow through and to use your legs to generate spin. This can be a great offensive shot if your opponent doesn't move very well. Flat shots are allowed but this drill is most effectively done with top spin.

Hitting over the rope alternating forehand and backhand down the line

For this drill you should hit over the rope with top spin with your forehand down the line and then the following shot with your backhand down the line. Continue doing this for the remainder of the drill. Work on keeping the ball deep on the court. Make sure to focus on your follow through and to use your legs to generate spin. This can be a great offensive shot if your opponent doesn't move very well. Flat shots are allowed but this drill is most effectively done with top spin.

Hitting under the rope cross court forehands

For this drill you should hit under the rope with top spin or flat with your forehand cross court and have the ball land deep on the court. Make sure to focus on your follow through and to use your legs to generate spin. This can be a great offensive shot if your opponent has a weaker forehand than you. Flat shots are allowed but this drill is most effectively done with top spin.

Hitting under the rope cross court backhands

For this drill you should hit under the rope with top spin or flat with your backhand cross court and have the ball land deep on the court. Make sure to focus on your follow through and to use your legs to generate spin. This can be a great offensive shot if your opponent has a weaker backhand than you. Flat shots are allowed but this drill is most effectively done with top spin.

Hitting under the rope down the line forehands

For this drill you should hit under the rope with top spin or flat with your forehand down the line and have the ball land deep on the court. Make sure to focus on your follow through and to use your legs to generate spin. This can be a great offensive shot if your opponent has a weak backhand. Flat shots are allowed but this drill is most effectively done with top spin.

Hitting under the rope down the line backhands

For this drill you should hit under the rope with top spin or flat with your backhand down the line and have the ball land deep on the court. Make sure to focus on your follow through and to use your legs to generate spin. This can be a great offensive shot if your opponent has a weak forehand on the run. Flat shots are allowed but this drill is most effectively done with top spin.

Hitting under the rope alternating forehands and backhands cross court

For this drill you should hit under the rope with top spin with your forehand cross court and then the following shot with your backhand cross court. Continue doing this for the remainder of the drill. Work on keeping the ball deep on the court. Make sure to focus on your follow through and to use your legs to generate spin. This can be a great offensive shot if your opponent doesn't move very well. Flat shots are allowed but this drill is most effectively done with top spin.

Hitting under the rope alternating forehands and backhands down the line

For this drill you should hit under the rope with top spin with your forehand down the line and then the following shot with your backhand down the line. Continue doing this for the remainder of the drill. Work on keeping the ball deep on the court. Make sure to focus on your follow through and to use your legs to generate spin. This can be a great offensive shot if your opponent doesn't move very well. Flat shots are allowed but this drill is most effectively done with top spin.

CHAPTER 7: LIVE BALL DRILLS

OVER THE ROPE

Over the rope 20 balls with topspin forehand to forehand cross court rally (consistency)

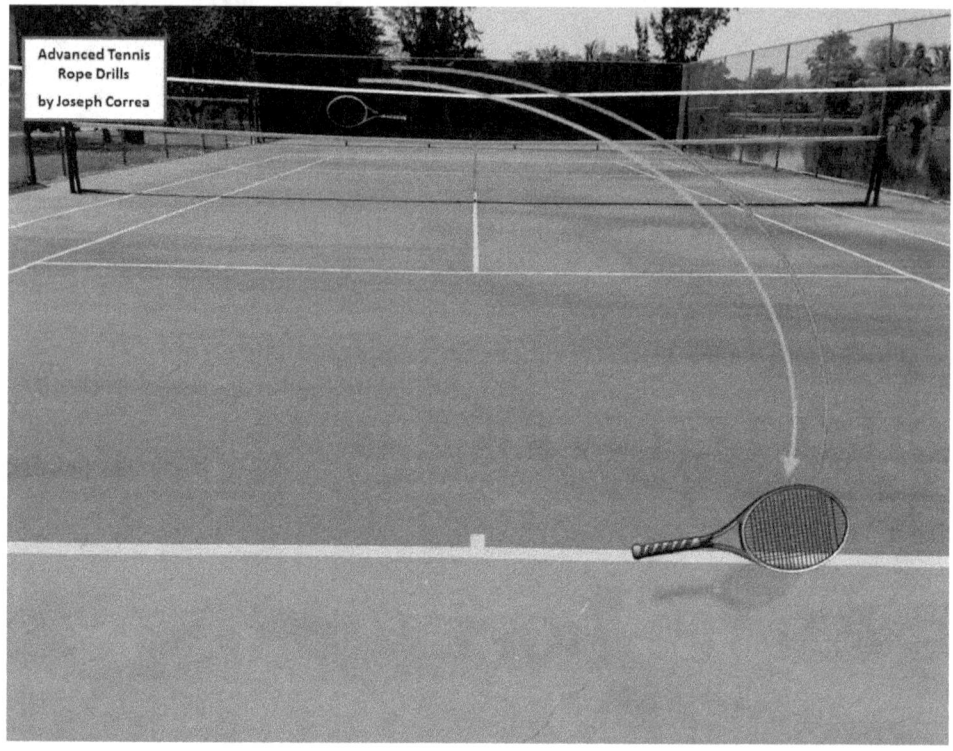

For this drill you should hit over the rope with top spin or flat with your forehand cross court and have the ball land deep on the court. Your hitting partner or coach should hit back cross court forehands to you. Your goal is to reach a minimum of 20 balls hit back and forth without missing. If you miss you have to start back at zero. Continue until you get passed 20 balls hit with this pattern. Flat shots are allowed but this drill is most effectively done with top spin.

Over the rope 20 balls with topspin backhand to backhand crosscourt rally (consistency)

For this drill you should hit over the rope with top spin or flat with your backhand cross court and have the ball land deep on the court. Your hitting partner or coach should hit back cross court backhands to you. Your goal is to reach a minimum of 20 balls hit back and forth without missing. If you miss you have to start back at zero. Continue until you get passed 20 balls hit with this pattern. Flat shots are allowed but this drill is most effectively done with top spin.

Over the rope 20 balls with topspin forehand to backhand down the line rally (consistency)

For this drill you should hit over the rope with top spin or flat with your forehand down the line and have the ball land deep on the court. Your hitting partner or coach should hit back down the line backhands to you. Your goal is to reach a minimum of 20 balls hit back and forth without missing. If you miss you have to start back at zero. Continue until you get passed 20 balls hit with this pattern. Flat shots are allowed but this drill is most effectively done with top spin.

Over the rope 20 balls with topspin backhand to forehand down the line rally (consistency)

For this drill you should hit over the rope with top spin or flat with your backhand down the line and have the ball land deep on the court. Your hitting partner or coach should hit back down the line forehands to you. Your goal is to reach a minimum of 20 balls hit back and forth without missing. If you miss you have to start back at zero. Continue until you get passed 20 balls hit with this pattern. Flat shots are allowed but this drill is most effectively done with top spin.

Over the rope 20 balls with one person hitting only cross court while the other does down the line shots (figure 8 consistency)

For this drill you should hit over the rope with top spin or flat with your forehand cross court and have the ball land deep on the court. Your hitting partner or coach should hit back down the line to your backhand. You now hit cross court to their backhand where they will return a down the line backhand to your forehand. This sequence will continue. Your goal is to reach a minimum of 20 balls hit back and forth without missing. Each ball hit counts as 1. If you miss you have to start back at zero. Continue until you get passed 20 balls hit with this pattern. Flat shots are allowed but this drill is most effectively done with top spin.

Over the rope 20 balls with one person hitting only down the line while the other does cross court shots (figure 8 consistency)

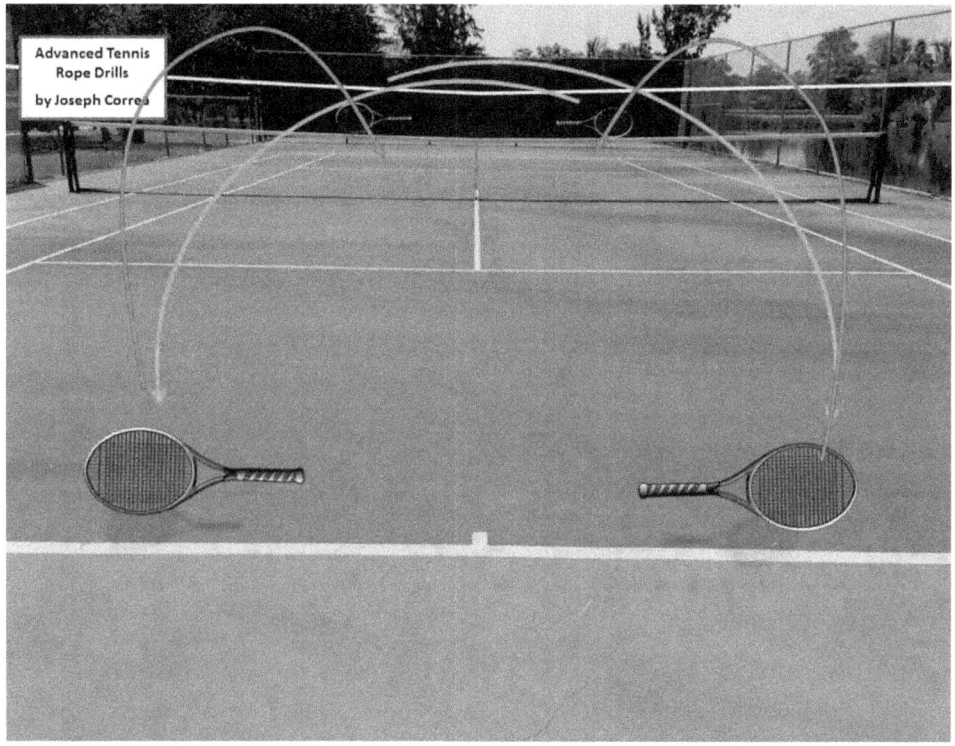

For this drill you should hit over the rope with top spin or flat with your forehand down the line and have the ball land deep on the court. Your hitting partner or coach should hit back cross court to your backhand. You now hit down the line to their backhand and they will return cross court to your forehand. This sequence will continue. Your goal is to reach a minimum of 20 balls hit back and forth without missing. Each ball hit counts as 1. If you miss you have to start back at zero. Continue until you get passed 20 balls hit with this pattern. Flat shots are allowed but this drill is most effectively done with top spin.

UNDER THE ROPE DRILLS

Under the rope 20 balls cross court forehand to forehand rally

For this drill you should hit under the rope with top spin or flat with your forehand cross court and have the ball land deep on the court. Your hitting partner or coach should hit back cross court forehands to you. Your goal is to reach a minimum of 20 balls hit back and forth without missing. If you miss you have to start back at zero. Continue until you get passed 20 balls hit with this pattern. Flat shots are allowed but this drill is most effectively done with top spin.

Under the rope 20 balls cross court backhand to backhand rally

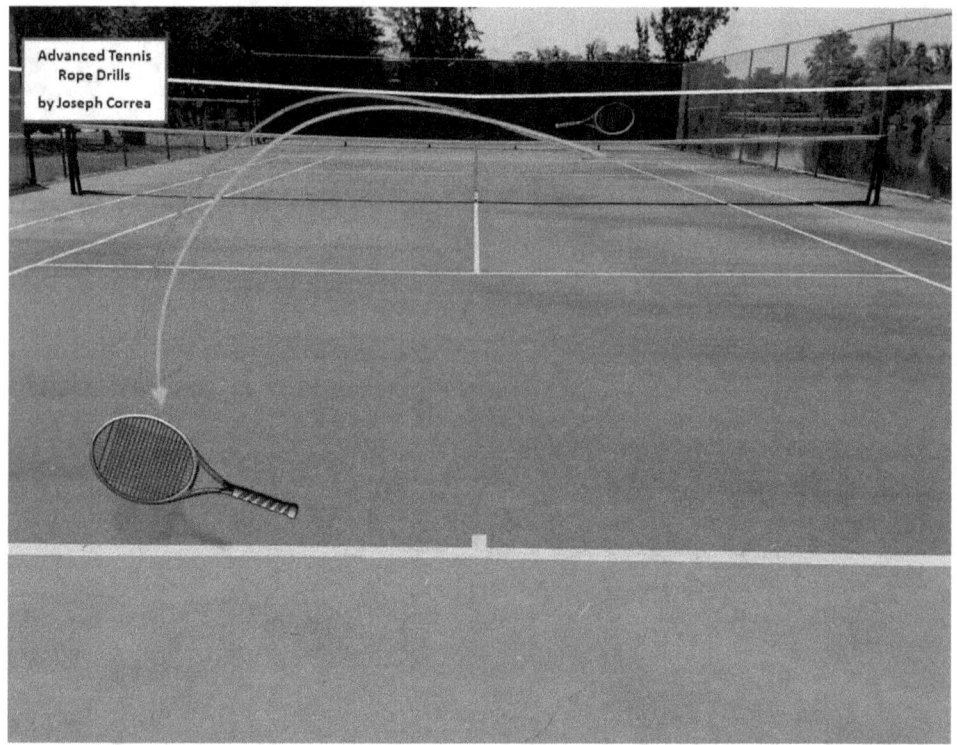

For this drill you should hit under the rope with top spin or flat with your backhand cross court and have the ball land deep on the court. Your hitting partner or coach should hit back cross court backhands to you. Your goal is to reach a minimum of 20 balls hit back and forth without missing. If you miss you have to start back at zero. Continue until you get passed 20 balls hit with this pattern. Flat shots are allowed but this drill is most effectively done with top spin.

Under the rope 20 balls down the line forehand to backhand rally

For this drill you should hit under the rope with top spin or flat with your forehand down the line and have the ball land deep on the court. Your hitting partner or coach should hit back down the line backhands to you. Your goal is to reach a minimum of 20 balls hit back and forth without missing. If you miss you have to start back at zero. Continue until you get passed 20 balls hit with this pattern. Flat shots are allowed but this drill is most effectively done with top spin.

Under the rope 20 balls down the line backhand to forehand rally

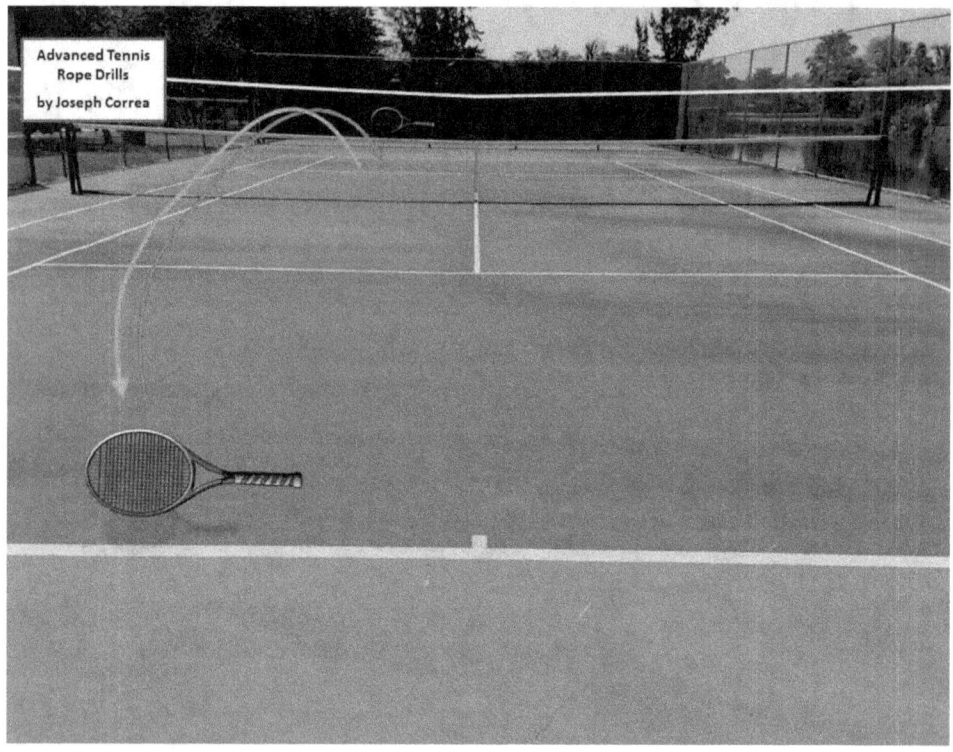

For this drill you should hit under the rope with top spin or flat with your backhand down the line and have the ball land deep on the court. Your hitting partner or coach should hit back down the line forehands to you. Your goal is to reach a minimum of 20 balls hit back and forth without missing. If you miss you have to start back at zero. Continue until you get passed 20 balls hit with this pattern. Flat shots are allowed but this drill is most effectively done with top spin.

Under the rope 20 balls cross court slice backhand rally

For this drill you should hit under the rope with slice with your backhand cross court and your hitting partner or coach should hit back slice cross court. Your goal is to reach a minimum of 20 balls hit back and forth without missing. If you miss you have to start back at zero. Continue until you get passed 20 balls hit with this pattern.

Under the rope 20 balls with one person hitting cross court while the other hits only down the line to create a figure 8

For this drill you should hit under the rope with top spin or flat with your forehand cross court. Your hitting partner or coach should hit back down the line to your backhand. You now hit cross court to their backhand where they will return a down the line backhand to your forehand. This sequence will continue. Your goal is to reach a minimum of 20 balls hit back and forth without missing. Each ball hit counts as 1. If you miss you have to start back at zero. Continue until you get passed 20 balls hit with this pattern. Flat shots are allowed but this drill is most effectively done with top spin.

Under the rope 20 balls with one person hitting down the line while the other hits only cross court to create a figure 8

For this drill you should hit under the rope with top spin or flat with your forehand down the line and have the ball land deep on the court. Your hitting partner or coach should hit back cross court to your backhand. You now hit down the line to their backhand and they will return cross court to your forehand. This sequence will continue. Your goal is to reach a minimum of 20 balls hit back and forth without missing. Each ball hit counts as 1. If you miss you have to start back at zero. Continue until you get passed 20 balls hit with this pattern. Flat shots are allowed but this drill is most effectively done with top spin.

OVER AND UNDER THE ROPE DRILLS

One person hits forehands over the rope with topspin while the person hits forehands under the rope cross court

For this drill you should hit over the rope with top spin or flat with your forehand cross court and have the ball land deep on the court. Your hitting partner or coach should hit back cross court forehands under the rope back to you. Your goal is to reach a minimum of 20 balls hit back and forth without missing. If you miss you have to start back at zero. Continue until you get passed 20 balls hit with this pattern. Flat shots are allowed but this drill is most effectively done with top spin.

One person hits backhands over the rope with topspin while the person hits backhands under the rope cross court

For this drill you should hit over the rope with top spin or flat with your backhand cross court and have the ball land deep on the court. Your hitting partner or coach should hit back cross court backhands under the rope back to you. Your goal is to reach a minimum of 20 balls hit back and forth without missing. If you miss you have to start back at zero. Continue until you get passed 20 balls hit with this pattern. Flat shots are allowed but this drill is most effectively done with top spin.

One person hits forehands over the rope with topspin while the person hits backhands under the rope down the line

For this drill you should hit over the rope with top spin or flat with your forehand down the line and have the ball land deep on the court. Your hitting partner or coach should hit back down the line backhands under the rope back to you. Your goal is to reach a minimum of 20 balls hit back and forth without missing. If you miss you have to start back at zero. Continue until you get passed 20 balls hit with this pattern. Flat shots are allowed but this drill is most effectively done with top spin.

One person hits backhands over the rope with topspin while the person hits forehands under the rope down the line

For this drill you should hit over the rope with top spin or flat with your backhand down the line and have the ball land deep on the court. Your hitting partner or coach should hit back down the line forehands under the rope back to you. Your goal is to reach a minimum of 20 balls hit back and forth without missing. If you miss you have to start back at zero. Continue until you get passed 20 balls hit with this pattern. Flat shots are allowed but this drill is most effectively done with top spin.

One person hits backhands over the rope with topspin while the person hits slice backhands under the rope cross court

For this drill you should hit over the rope with top spin or flat with your backhand cross court and have the ball land deep on the court. Your hitting partner or coach should hit back cross court slices under the rope back to you. Your goal is to reach a minimum of 20 balls hit back and forth without missing. If you miss you have to start back at zero. Continue until you get passed 20 balls hit with this pattern. Flat shots are allowed but this drill is most effectively done with top spin.

One person hits forehands over the rope with topspin while the person hits forehands under the rope crosscourt inside out

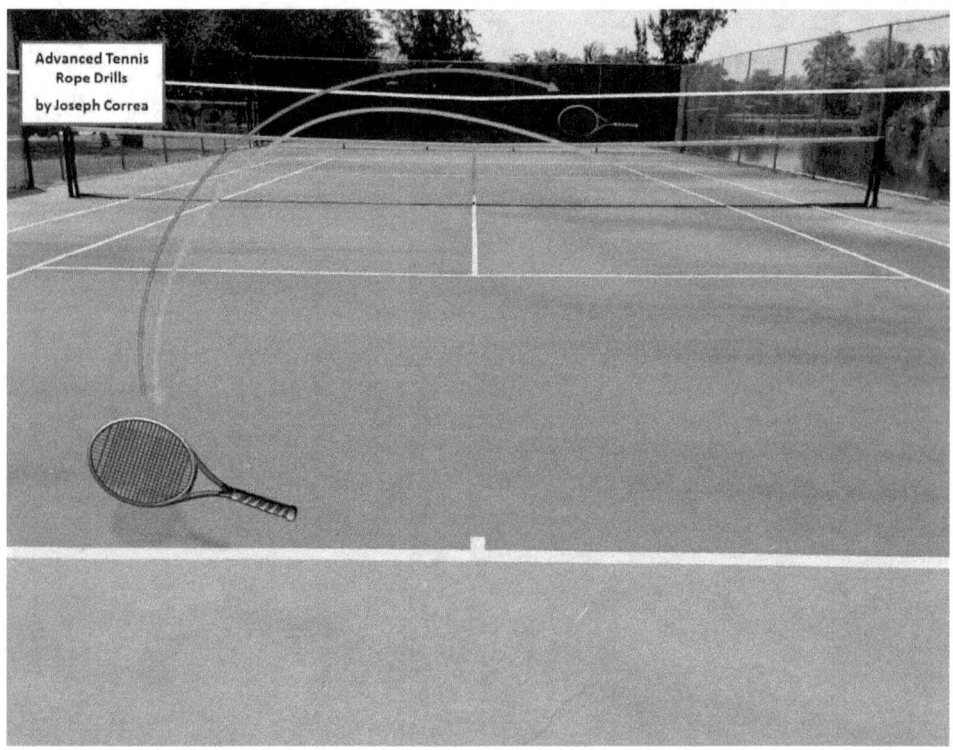

For this drill you should hit over the rope with top spin or flat with your forehand down the line from the backhand corner and have the ball land deep on the court. Your hitting partner or coach should hit back down the line forehands under the rope back to you. Your goal is to reach a minimum of 20 balls hit back and forth without missing. If you miss you have to start back at zero. Continue until you get passed 20 balls hit with this pattern. Flat shots are allowed but this drill is most effectively done with top spin.

CHAPTER 8: POINT DRILLS

Points up to 10 only over the rope without serve

Play up to 10 points with the winner reaching 10 while hitting only over the rope.

Points up to 10 only under the rope without serve

Play up to 10 points with the winner reaching 10 while hitting only under the rope.

Points up to 10 where one person can only hit over the rope while the other can only hit under the rope without serve

Play up to 10 points with the winner reaching 10 while hitting only over the rope for one person and under the rope for the other person.

Points up to 10 (with serve) over the rope (serve goes under the rope at all times unless you are doing topspin or kick serve)

Play up to 10 points with the winner reaching 10 while hitting only over the rope and starting the point with a serve that should always go under the rope.

Points up to 10 (with serve) under the rope (serve goes under the rope at all times unless you are doing topspin or kick serve)

Play up to 10 points with the winner reaching 10 while hitting only under the rope and starting the point with a serve that should always go under the rope.

CHAPTER 9: NORMAL POINT DRILLS WITHOUT ROPE

37. Points up the 10 without serve only cross court forehands

Feed the ball under hand to your opponent's forehand and then play the point cross court only as to have both of you hitting only cross court until one of you wins the point with a winner or one of you misses and hits to the net or out. Remember that if one or both of you are left handed please make the necessary adjustments to this drill. The first person to reach 10 points wins. There is no "difference of two points" structure in these drills.

38. Points up to 10 without serve only cross court backhands

Feed the ball under hand to your opponent's backhand and then play the point cross court only as to have both of you hitting only cross court until one of you wins the point with a winner or one of you misses and hits to the net or out. Remember that if one or both of you are left handed please make the necessary adjustments to this drill. The first person to reach 10 points wins. There is no "difference of two points" structure in these drills.

39. Points up to 10 without serve only down the line backhand to forehand

Feed the ball under hand to your opponent's forehand and then play the point down the line only as to have both of you hitting until one of you wins the point with a winner or one of you misses and hits to the net or out. Remember that if one or both of you are left handed please make the necessary adjustments to this drill. The first person to reach 10 points wins. There is no "difference of two points" structure in these drills.

40. Points up the 10 without serve only down the line forehand to backhand

Feed the ball under hand to your opponent's backhand and then play the point down the line only as to have both of you hitting until one of you wins the point with a winner or one of you misses and hits to the net or out. Remember that if one or both of you are left handed please make the necessary adjustments to this drill. The first person to reach 10 points wins. There is no "difference of two points" structure in these drills.

41. Points up the 10 with serve only cross court forehands

Serve the ball to your opponent's forehand and then play the point cross court only as to have both of you hitting only cross court until one of you wins the point with a winner or one of you misses and hits to the net or out. Remember that if one or both of you are left handed please make the necessary adjustments to this drill. The first person to reach 10 points wins. There is no "difference of two points" structure in these drills.

42. Points up to 10 with serve only cross court backhands

Serve the ball to your opponent's backhand and then play the point cross court only as to have both of you hitting only cross court until one of you wins the point with a winner or one of you misses and hits to the net or out. Remember that if one or both of you are left handed please make the necessary adjustments to this drill. The first person to reach 10 points wins. There is no "difference of two points" structure in these drills.

43. Points up to 10 with serve only down the line backhand to forehand

Serve the ball to your opponent's forehand and then play the point down the line only as to have both of you hitting until one of you wins the point with a winner or one of you misses and hits to the net or out. Remember that if one or both of you are left handed please make the necessary adjustments to this drill. The first person to reach 10 points wins. There is no "difference of two points" structure in these drills.

44. Points up the 10 with serve only down the line forehand to backhand

Serve the ball to your opponent's backhand and then play the point down the line only as to have both of you hitting until one of you wins the point with a winner or one of you misses and hits to the net or out. Remember that if one or both of you are left handed please make the necessary adjustments to this drill. The first person to reach 10 points wins. There is no "difference of two points" structure in these drills.

45. Points up to 10 where one person can only hit cross court and the other person can only hit down the line without serve

Feed the ball under hand to your opponent's forehand and then play the point cross court only as to have both of you hitting only cross court until one of you wins the point with a winner or one of you misses and hits to the net or out. Remember that if one or both of you are left handed please make the necessary adjustments to this drill. The first person to reach 10 points wins. There is no "difference of two points" structure in these drills.

46. Points up to 10 where one person can only hit down the line and the other person can only hit cross court without serve

Feed the ball under hand to your opponent's forehand and then play the point cross court only as to have both of you hitting only cross court until one of you wins the point with a winner or one of you misses and hits to the net or out. Remember that if one or both of you are left handed please make the necessary adjustments to this drill. The first person to reach 10 points wins. There is no "difference of two points" structure in these drills.

47. Points up to 10 where one person can only hit cross court and the other person can only hit down the line with serve

Serve the ball to your opponent and then play the point cross court while your partner hits only down the line as to create a figure 8. Keep the ball in play until one of you wins the point with a winner or one of you misses and hits to the net or out. Remember that if one or both of you are left handed please make the necessary adjustments to this drill. The first person to reach 10 points wins. There is no "difference of two points" structure in these drills.

48. Points up to 10 where one person can only hit down the line and the other person can only hit cross court with serve

Serve the ball to your opponent and then play the point cross court while your partner hits only down the line as to create a figure 8. Keep the ball in play until one of you wins the point with a winner or one of you misses and hits to the net or out. Remember that if one or both of you are left handed please make the necessary adjustments to this drill. The first person to reach 10 points wins. There is no "difference of two points" structure in these drills.

49. Points up to 10 without serve. Complete normal points without any patterns.

Feed the ball to your opponent under hand and then play the point normally without any required patterns. Keep the ball in play until one of you wins the point with a winner or one of you misses and hits to the net or out. Remember that if one or both of you are left handed please make the necessary adjustments to this drill. The first person to reach 10 points wins. There is no "difference of two points" structure in these drills.

50. Points up to 10 with serve. Complete normal points without any patterns.

Serve the ball to your opponent and then play the point without any required patterns. Keep the ball in play until one of you wins the point with a winner or one of you misses and hits to the net or out. Remember that if one or both of you are left handed please make the necessary adjustments to this drill. The first person to reach 10 points wins. There is no "difference of two points" structure in these drills.

51. Play a complete set with serve playing only cross court while your partner hits only down the line.

52. Play a complete set with serve playing only down the line while your partner hits only cross court.

53. Play a complete set using any pattern you desire.

54. Play a complete match using any pattern you desire.

WOULD YOU DO ME A FAVOR?

Thank you for downloading and reading this book. I hope it was helpful and at least one thing makes you win an extra match or two.

I have a small favor to ask. Would you mind writing a short comment and rate this book?

I like to read all the reviews on my books and enjoy knowing what others think of this book. I feel the best pay comes from good positive reviews from tennis enthusiasts that enjoyed reading it.

You can complete your review on Amazon.com or on Ibookstore.
If you know of a family member or friend, that you think would benefit from reading this book, please take a minute to share it with them so that they may improve their game as well. I enjoy helping others and would like to answer questions free of charge. You can Tweet me on www.twitter.com at @mybetterswing.com
Check out some of my other books on the next page.

OTHER TITLES BY JOSEPH CORREA

Tennis Serve Harder Training Program

This DVD will teach you how to serve 10-20 mph faster in a 3 month day by day program. The best serve training program in the market. Video includes a 3 month chart training program and a step by step manual. The DVD shows you how to do the exercises properly and the process you should follow in order to be successful with the program.

Joseph Correa is a professional tennis player and coach that has competed and taught all over the world in ITF and ATP tournaments for many years. Besides being a professional tennis player he has a USPTR professional coaching certification and ITF kids coaching certification.

The 33 Laws of Tennis

The 33 Laws of Tennis is book full of valuable tennis concepts to help you become a better and more prepared tennis player. It was written by a professional tennis player and coach in the USA. It's a very useful book that will come in handy when you least expect it and will remind you of many little but important things before competing.

Tennis Footwork and Cardio by Joseph Correa

Joseph Correa is a professional tennis player and coach that has competed and taught all over the world in ITF and ATP tournaments for many years. Besides being a professional tennis player he has a USPTR professional coaching certification and ITF kids coaching certification.

Get in better shape and improve your mobility on and off

the tennis court. Your foot work will improve drastically as well as strengthen your core and upper body. This is definitely worthwhile for a serious tennis player no matter what your level. You become faster, stronger, and more agile and on the court as well as seeing an increase in acceleration in your groundstrokes and serve. Created by a professional tennis player for others to advance in their game and win more matches.

Yoga Tennis by Joseph Correa
Yoga Tennis by Joseph Correa is a great way to improve your flexibility and agility on the court. Reach more balls and have fewer injuries. It's a great way to win more by working on a different part of your game. The DVD lasts about 30 minutes. Used by amateur and professional tennis players to improve their game and last longer in matches. This is the best way for a tennis player to become more flexible and get rid of common back, knee, shoulder, hamstring, calf, and quadriceps injuries. You´ll be glad to get started! This is an improved version of our MBS Yoga Tennis 2012.

The Vilcabamba Diet
The best diet and exercise book you will find if you want to get in shape and live longer. It's based on a village in Ecuador called "Vilcabamba" where most of its inhabitants live longer than the average person and in great condition. Great for athletes!

Tennis Abs by Joseph Correa
Tennis Abs is a great way to strengthen your core for more powerful serves, forehands and backhands as well as stronger volleys. Abdominals are fundamental for a better game. This DVD works on many types of crunches,

sit-ups, and lateral abs and back exercises that you won´t find in other abdominal videos. Feel confident when changing your shirt during your match and hit the ball harder!

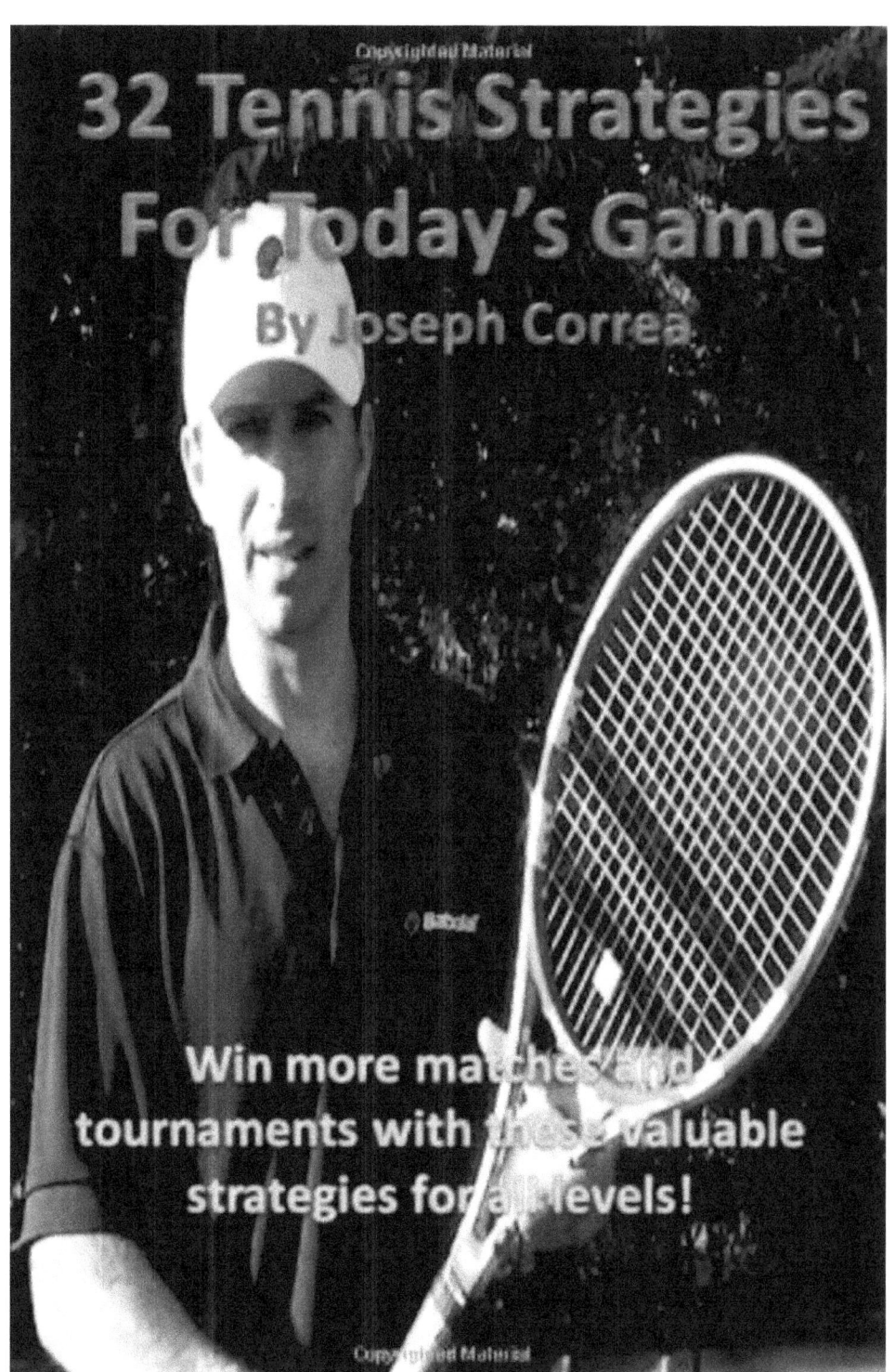

THE 33 LAWS OF TENNIS

Thirty three concepts to improve your game

By Joseph Correa

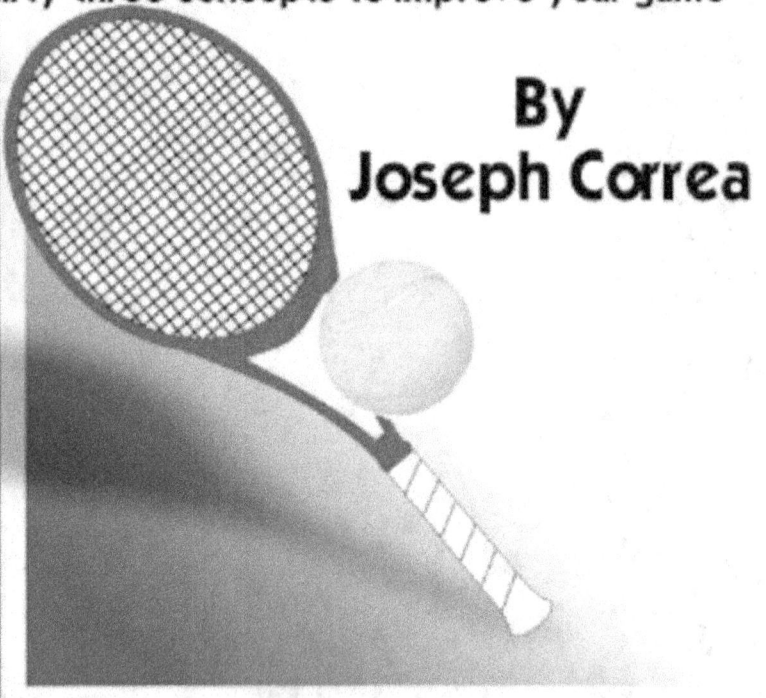

Actual professionals share their trade secrets in this highly practical guide to becoming the best tennis player you can be.

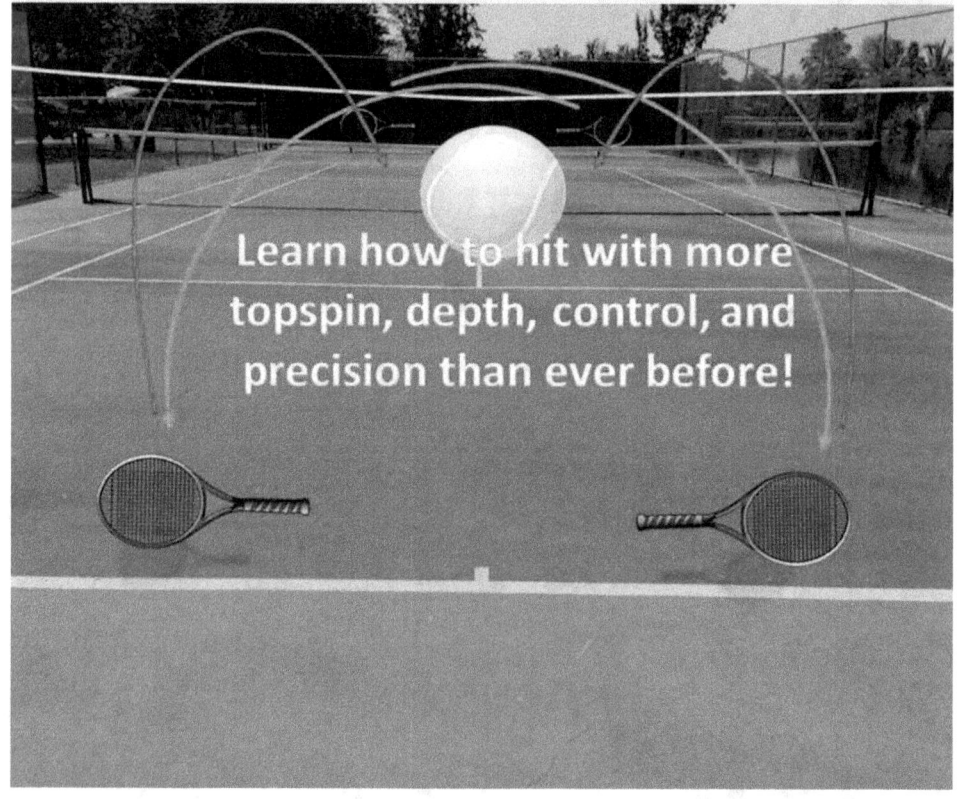

Superman Tennis Serve

Learn how to serve your fastest serve ever through scientifically proven techniques!

By Joseph Correa

DR. JUAN CARLOS CORREA and JOSEPH CORREA

The Vilcabamba Diet :

Lose 10 pounds or more!

Lose Weight, Live Longer, and Eat Healthier with the Magic Formula of our Ancestors

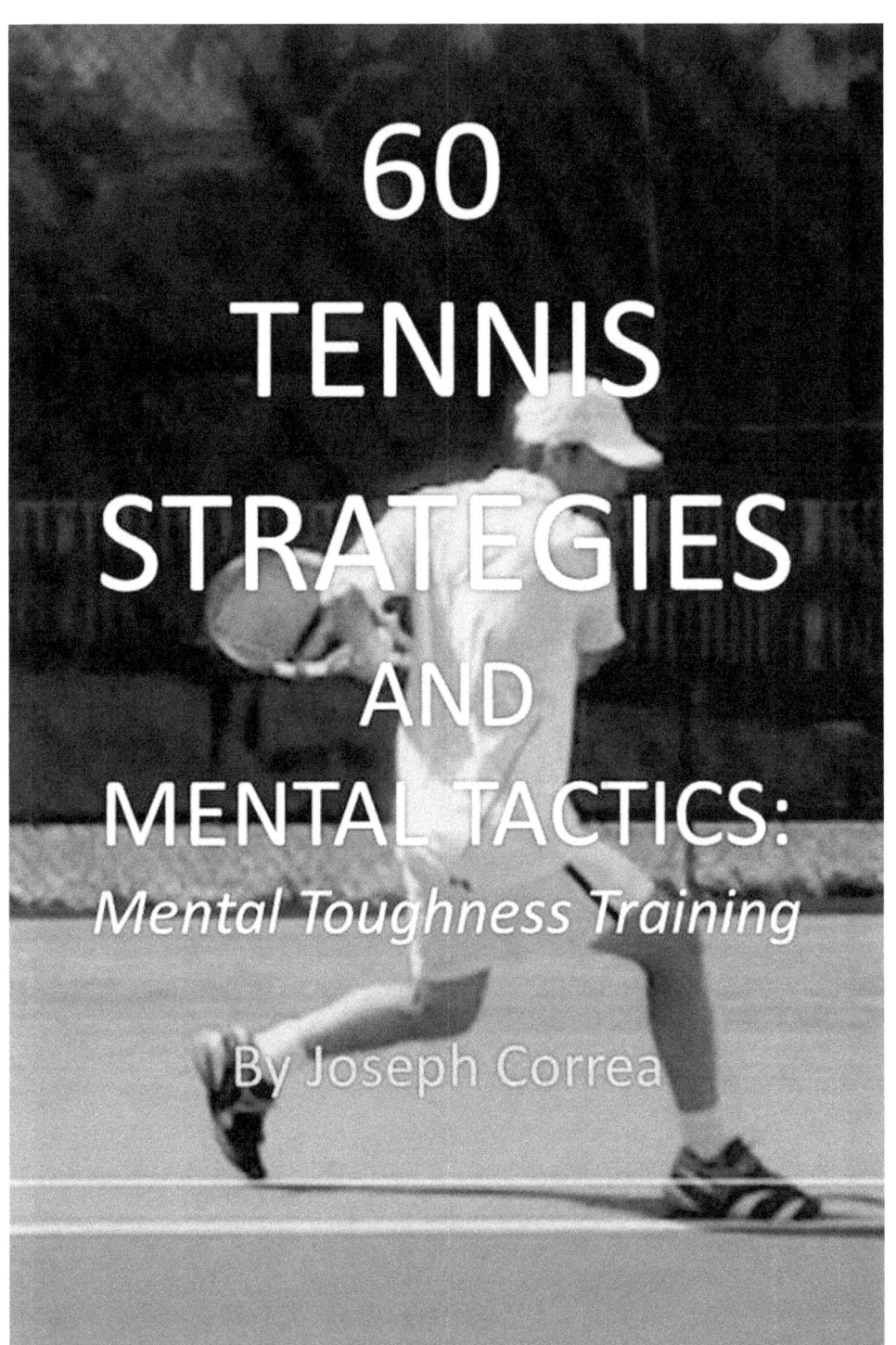

60 TENNIS STRATEGIES AND MENTAL TACTICS:
Mental Toughness Training

By Joseph Correa

www.ingramcontent.com/pod-product-compliance
Lightning Source LLC
Chambersburg PA
CBHW071159070526
44584CB00019B/2855